NORTHAMPTON

—— Images of Wartime ——

First Published in Great Britain by
Jones-Sands Publishing 1994, Coventry

ISBN 0-947764-76-3

To preserve the quality and character, the pictures in this publication
have not been re-touched in any way.

This book was designed by:-

Jones-Sands Publishing
8 Trimley Close
Upton
Wirral
L49 6PQ
England
Tele/Fax (0151 606 0240)

Typeset in Great Britain by Jones-Sands Publishing

Printed by M.E. Wilkinson Ltd, Nuneaton, England

Marketed and distributed by Jones-Sands Publishing

NORTHAMPTON

Images of Wartime

Alan Burman

Cyril Arnold as a young press photographer recorded
many of the principal events of the war at home

Preparations for war began long before 1939. As early as 1937 Northamptonians had a chance to inspect an array of armoured vehicles at the Drill Hall. The aim was to recruit volunteers for the "Terriers", the army reserve.

INTRODUCTION

Northampton was not in the front line of World War II. It was not blitzed, it was not ringed with airfields or large army camps, nor was it the springboard for the D-Day offensive. Nevertheless, the events of those wartime years are etched into the memory of those who were left to cope at home and the children who grew up in those dark days.

Speaking for the children, we did not feel deprived. Sure, there were few sweets, food was basic, and foreign fruits, particularly bananas unobtainable, but every day was exciting; new happenings all around.

Of course, it was different for adults. Beset by the trials of everyday existence, they had the added worry of husbands, sweethearts and loved ones serving in some distant theatre of war and not knowing what was happening to them.

The major campaigns of the war have been comprehensively illustrated by official photographers. The home front was not so well covered. Photographic materials, film, and so on, were almost unobtainable for amateur use, professional photographers were mostly male and away at war, but in any case supplies of sensitized materials and chemicals were limited.

As it was recognised that newspapers had an important morale-boosting role to play, press photographers, who had to be licensed by the Ministry of Information, had more freedom than most to capture the passing scene. Even so, every picture taken had to be submitted to censors who scrutinised it for anything that might be of importance to the enemy. The caption was studied and specific information and locations deleted with the proverbial blue pencil. Northampton became "Somewhere in England"! The photograph was then returned bearing the official stamp of approval or a slip banning publication altogether. A number of the pictures used in this book are of the latter type and are here published for the first time.

Strangely, the pictures do not reflect the photographers difficulties in obtaining them. Travel was restricted. A man with a camera, of serving age, and wearing civilian clothes, was viewed with suspicion. He might be a spy! Frequently the cameraman was detained and his equipment confiscated until his identity could be established.

Most of the photographs in this book were taken by Cyril Arnold who joined the Chronicle & Echo in 1938 and whose experience as a press photographer spanned twenty years. After war service and injury in the operation that ended at Dunkirk, he was invalided out of the army and returned to his former occupation, recording the wartime scene in and around Northampton.

I am grateful to the Chronicle & Echo for access to their library and permission to use certain key pictures.

As it is, these rare surviving photographs serve as a tribute to the Northampton folk who "kept the home fires burning"..

Alan Burman

Above: The Munich crisis in September of 1938 sharpened everyones awareness of the imminence of war. Immediately work was put in hand digging trenches in expectation of air attack. Deeper concrete shelters were also constructed in local parks, like this one on the Racecourse, of a type designed and preconstructed by Bells, the local fireplace manufacturers.

Left: The insides did not stay as clean and tidy as this for long, however. They rapidly became damp, smelly, and decidedly unhygienic!

Above: In 1938 National Defence had become Air Raid Precautions under Sir John Anderson. Public buildings and ARP depots, like this First Aid Post on the Racecourse, were shrouded in sandbags. From left to right can be seen, Chief Constable John Williamson, Mr H.C. Perrin billeting officer, Mr R.A. Winfield assistant controller, Inspector Cookson, Nurse King, Mr E. Dunkley, Sister E.M. Mason, Private Wootton, Dr.S. Rowland medical officer, Counc.S. Adnitt, Corporal Desborough, and Dr. James Orr.

Above: Surface shelters sprang up in practically every street. Due to an incorrect mix of mortar 75% of them fell down at the first heavy rains, raising a great scandal. They were all rebuilt using a strong cement mix.

Above: At the Northampton Town & County Grammar School, in Billing Road, the Officer Training Corps was mobilised. In this pre-war picture the boys, though having no uniforms, have real rifles.

Below: On this subsequent, wartime, occasion when they paraded at Overstone Park before Lt-Gen.G. St. G. Robinson they had acquired proper uniforms, but had lost their rifles and had to make do with wooden makeshifts.

Left: Foremost among the campaigners for appeasement was pacifist Stanley Seamark, seen here demonstrating outside the United Counties bus station in Derngate at the height of the war.

Right: Not all Northamptonians were in support of Britain's stance and conscientious objectors paraded with placards.

Below: By 1939 over a million and a half men and women had volunteered for A.R.P. duties countrywide. Squads of specialists had been set up like this unit "somewhere in Northampton" seen trying out their newly issued service-type gas masks. By the outbreak of war everyone had been issued with a mask of suitable type and, on September 3rd, 1939, it became compulsory to carry it at all times. The letters on the steel helmets indicate "Rescue" or "Decontamination" squads.

Above: Recruiting was also being vigorously pursued at the Drill Hall where a visiting unit of the Tank Corps was on public display.

Right: A trial blackout of all external lights was held August 9th, 1939. At the bottom of Gold Street a Gas Company workman turns off a street lamp. The traffic lights have already been blanked off and the lorry has the bulb removed from the nearside headlamp and a mask on the offside one. Two days before the declaration of war total blackout was enforced.

Left: Local children got a personal guide in the person of Major-General Sir John Brown who was then in charge of the Territorial Army.

Above: Ammunition was dispersed throughout the country and stored in the corrugated iron shelters that lined the verges of country lanes, like these seen at Great Billing.

Left: Sights like the brilliantly lit front-of-house of the Tivoli Cinema, in Far Cotton, would not be seen again until the end of the war.

Left: To avoid accidents in the blackout street kerbs, lamp-posts, etc. were painted white. An Austin taxi belonging to Nortax has its bumper painted. The edges of the running boards and mudguards were next to be given a white border.

Above: On May 10th 1940 Chamberlain resigned as Prime Minister. Churchill took over the coalition government. That same month the formation of the Local Defence Volunteers was announced. Immediately the authorities were swamped with applications. On 23rd July, with 1,300,000 enroled, the name was changed to the Home Guard. This group of LDV from the Northampton L.M.S. Railway group, being drilled by C.S.M. G. Quartermain, (a former Regimental Sergeant-Major who held the D.C.M. and the Military Medal (left)), and second-in-command R.J. Marfleet, (who had seen service in the previous war in the Royal Naval Air Service and the R.A.F. (right)), on duty guarding Far Cotton railway yard were lucky, they had real rifles. Many units had to patrol with broom-handles, pickaxe staves, and pitchforks!

Right: Sunday mornings and evenings were spent perfecting their reactions in the event of invasion. This included erecting PSI concrete road blocks located with lengths of railway line, as here at Spinney Hill.

Above: With the original
conscription extended to include
all men between 20 and 41, women
took over many public and service
jobs. The first Northampton
Corporation bus conductress, a
"clippie", was a great novelty.

Right: And soon women were
driving buses, too. This United
Counties driver is finding out how
it all works!

Left: Less than a month after war was declared, a scheme of National Registration was introduced and everyone was required to carry an identification card. Northamptonians had to get used to random checks, like this one on Kingsley Park Parade, which also examined documents relating to vehicle use and fuel allocation.

Below: Rationing was introduced on January 8th, 1940. Three months later Lord Woolton, seen here during a visit to Kettering, became Minister of Food and tightened up food rationing to 2 oz of margarine or cooking fat, 2 oz tea, 4 oz butter, 4 oz cheese, and 1/10d (9p) worth of meat a week. "Woolton Pie", made mainly from potatoes, a few added vegetables, and oatmeal, was a nationally recommended dish..... and became something of a joke!

Left: Much of Northampton's Racecourse was obliterated by army buildings as it became a camp. Some of it housed A.T.S. personnel, seen here parading for the Princess Royal. Several drives were launched to raise money for munitions.

Below: Several drives were launched to raise money for munitions. War Weapons Week, in November 1940. The target was to raise £1,000,000 to pay for 50 bombers, but the final figure invested in war savings was £1,251,303, buying a total of 62 1/2. Throughout the week a great "Bombometer", a chart across the facade of the Emporium Arcade, was adjusted daily to indicate the progress of the campaign. One display saw this tank on the Market Square engulfed in a tidal wave of small boys .... probably a more terrifying confrontation than the crew would experience for the rest of the war!

Below: Men too old for armed service, or in reserved occupations, volunteered for the auxiliary services, ambulance, fire service, special constabulary, etc. They were required to undergo a medical examination at the Drill Hall.....

.... which included a chest X-ray (Right).

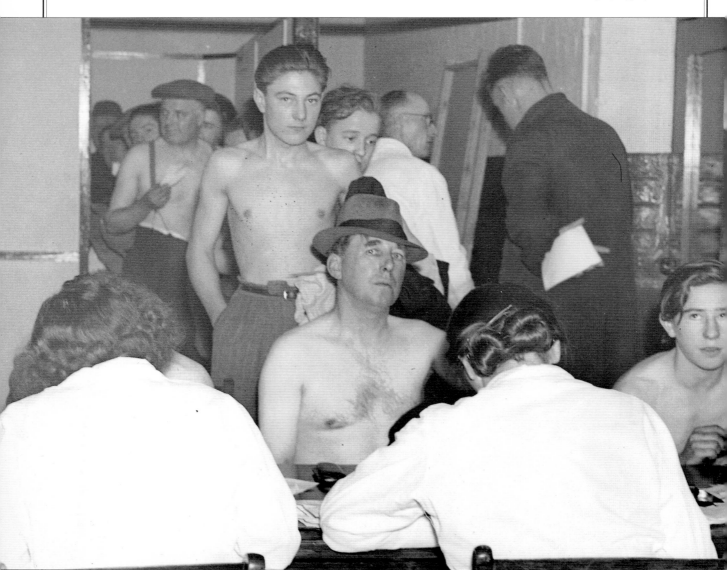

Right: Volunteers were called to give blood for storage. A team from the General Hospital travelled out to the villages to collect it. Dr. G.S. Sturtridge and his nurses in action at Paulerspury.

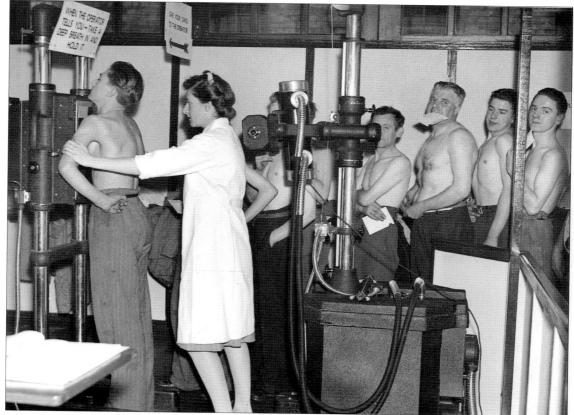

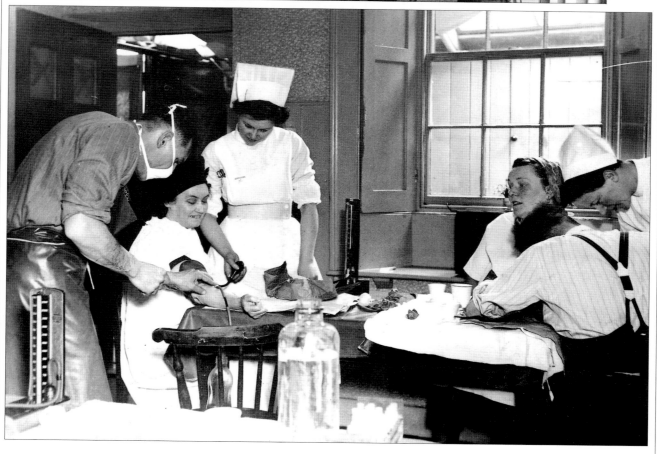

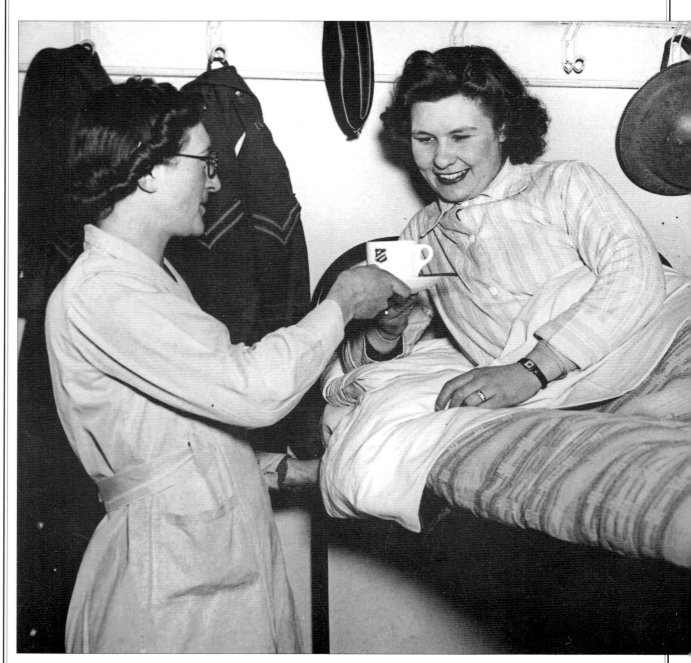

Above: Although Northampton was not an air-raid target, mock alerts kept people on their toes. An A.T.S. corporal in an emergency shelter in a local school hall gets a cup of tea in bed from a Salvation Army worker during a mock air-raid..... something she didn't get in camp!

Right: Less comfortable was a night on the floor of Vernon Terrace School. It, too, was an emergency air-raid shelter for people caught in the vicinity when the sirens sounded.

Above: As well as their daytime jobs, many folk also undertook night-time duties as "fire-watchers" and "roof-spotters", looking out for enemy raiders. These two are on the roof of the Police Station on the Mounts.

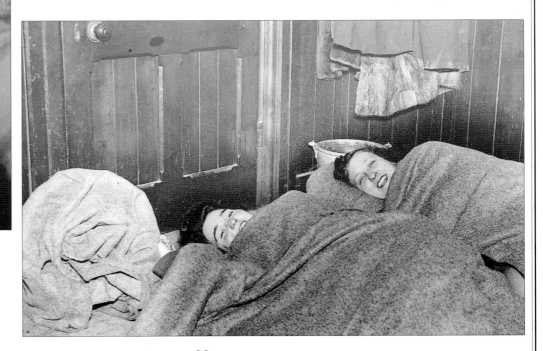

Above: Women drivers of the A.R.P. ambulance service were required to have a practical knowledge of motor mechanics. The working of a Northampton Corporation bus is explained during a training session at the United Counties depot on the Bedford Road.

Right: Northampton had had a relatively quiet time as far as air-raids were concerned, when, one January night in 1941, a German plane unloaded a stick of bombs across the town demolishing buildings at St. Andrews Hospital and leaving huge craters in Billing Road cemetery. Nearby residents had lucky escapes when tombstones came crashing through their roofs and landed on their beds.

Left: Rumour had it that the Nazi pilot had mistaken the glint of moonlight on the marble gravestones for a blacked-out munition factory!

Left: In April another random load of German bombs fell near Northampton demolishing storage sheds at Billing flax mills......

.... and overturning wagons on the railway line at Hardingstone (Below).

Right: In July of 1941
Northamptonians awoke to
discover their town centre littered
with broken masonry, wreckage,
and broken glass. It was not an
air raid, however, but a crashing
British craft that had caused it.
A four-engined Stirling bomber
returning crippled from a raid
was guided clear of the town by
the crew before they bailed out.
By a strange quirk of fate, the
plane circled before straightening
out and descending, dead in line
with Gold Street. The fuselage
hurtled up the centre of the street,
tearing the wings off and
scattering chunks of debris all
the way until it crashed in
George Row. Fire broke out
setting fire to All Saints church
doors, although bombs that
remained on board the craft
luckily did not explode. A large
quantity of machine-gun
ammunition went off ricocheting
off nearby buildings. The only
fatality was the pilot, whose
parachute failed to open. A
patrolling policeman, who was
blown off his bicycle by the blast,
suffered a broken leg. The scene
at the top of Gold Street. This
policeman regards the
photographer with a suspicious
eye..

There was not much left of the
aircraft, as this scene in
George Row shows, though the
bombs remained intact.

Above: The 25th of October, 1941, saw the opening of Warship Week by the First Lord of the Admiralty, A.V. Alexander (oddly, wearing the uniform of the Royal Squadron!) A mock battleship quarter-deck was built on the Market Square and dubbed HMS Payupansmyle. Money raised during the week payed for HMS Laforey, still looked upon by Northamptonians as their ship.

Right: By 1942, three years after it was founded, 61,000 women were engaged in agriculture as members of the Womens Land Army, a number which swelled to 200,000 by 1944. This buxom bunch march past the Town Hall on a Sunday morning church parade.

Right: In March 1941 a Registration for Employment Order for Women was passed for women 20 to 30, soon followed by an Essential Work 0rder which enabled them to be directed into war work. For the remainder of the war over 50% of workers in aircraft production and repair were women. These two girls in a local factory are working on a Flying Fortress.

Above: An elderly local farmer and a lad get a help-ing hand to get the harvest in from a couple of Land Army girls. It is not the neatest of loads, but hard-pushed farmers were grateful for the help of these women, who worked a 48 hour week for 28/= (£1.40p), out of which they had to pay for board and food at their hostels.

Right: Land Army girls not only worked on the farm, many were employed in forestry. In Hazelborough Woods, near Silverstone, a couple of women prepare felled timber for removal.

Left: The Duchess of Gloucester (left) recognised their vital war work when she visited a harvest celebration in the village hall at Titchmarsh, near Kettering.

Below: By 1942 rationing was rigorous. Each adult was allowed 8 oz sugar a week, 8 oz of fat, only 2 oz of which could be butter, the rest being margarine or cooking fat, 1/2d worth of meat, the odd 2d of which had be spent on corned beef, 2 oz of tea and 2 oz of cheese. White bread had long ago disappeared. The infamous powdered egg, imported from the U.S. to supplement "eggs in shell", became part of wartime recipes. Soap was rationed to 3 oz per month. Items off the ration were rare and much sought after, like tomatoes, which created this queue on the Market Square. Single bananas and onions were rare enough to figure as raffle prizes. In normal shops pregnant women were allowed to go to the head of the queue on production of a special ration book.

Right: As part of their war effort, staff of the Chronicle & Echo collected unwanted items and sold them on the Market Square to raise money to provide comforts for British prisoners of war. With trouser turn-ups, pleats, long socks, and pockets in womens suits banned, pre-war clothing was much in demand. Les Tatum, Harry Clarke, and George Eagle, alias the Jumble Brothers, in action.

Left: Early on a drive to promote greater fitness among women was launched which continued throughout the war. Keep Fit classes were held in many local school halls.

Below Left: At the Salon de Danse, at Franklin's Gardens, Madame Alwyn's Keep Fit Class was very popular, with dance exercises reminiscent of Prunella Stack's 1930s Womens League of Health and Beauty.

Below: Fund raising was going on apace. Lord Beaverbrook, Minister of Aircraft Production, launched Spitfire Funds and Northampton's was one of the first to take place. Having raised the necessary £5,000, a plane came off the production line carrying the name and arms of Northampton. Enough cash poured in to buy a similar fighter for the County with funds left over.

Above: Signing in at the Wellingborough "Day Club".

Left: On December 6th, 1941 the Japanese bombed Pearl Harbour. Five days later the U.S.A. declared war on Germany. Immediately, thousands of G.I.s were despatched to Britain the first arriving by January 1942. Not many local folk had even seen a black man and even fewer had come across segregation. Black American servicemen had their rest centres and leisure facilities in Wellingborough while Northampton was reserved for whites.

Right: Rest centres were set up for white G.I.s by the American Red Cross here, at the Plough Hotel in Bridge Street.

Black and white came together for a church service in the little parish church of Cransley.

Baseball was seen on the County Ground.....

.... and American football was played at Franklins Gardens.

Above: Local girls rallied round to
make the "Yanks" feel welcome. This
group of girls were regular visitors to
the American Red Cross Centre at the
Plough Hotel, Northampton. The boy
seated on the left is John Barrons, later
to become editor of the Chronicle &
Echo, centre is Mrs Ross Church, local
organiser of the American Red Cross,
while on the right can be seen sisters
Babs and Teddy, who entertained as part
of "The Coram Twins and Joy ", later to
become the Beverley Sisters.

Right: Anglo-American co-operation
sometimes had happy results, like this
Northampton girl's marriage.

Left: Regular outings to places of historical interest were arranged by the Northampton Friendship Committee for G.I.s who preferred something a bit more educational than the nightlife of Northampton! During a visit to Sulgrave Manor, the ancestral home of the Washington family, the editor of the Chronicle & Echo, Mr W. Cowper Barrons, addresses the party.

Above: Frequent group photographs were taken by the Chronicle & Echo and prints sent to the men's local newspapers in America. They were also reproduced as leaflets for the men to post home. Cyril Arnold is seen at work in Northampton's Guildhall.

Right: The Barratt Maternity Home was, at one point, nearly taken over by American fathers who well outnumbered local Dads. Nurses marked the trend by hanging out the appropriate flag.

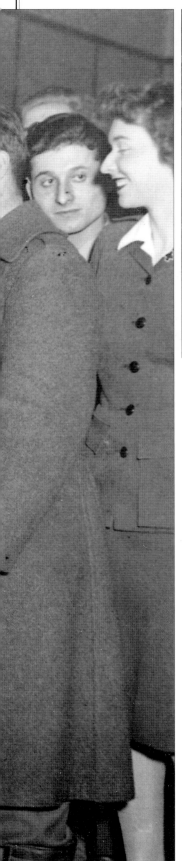

Left: Show business rallied round to keep morale up and those entertainers who were not enroled in E.N.S.A. visited servicemen locally. Noel Coward, during a break from his appearance at the New Theatre, amused Americans with his "terribly English" songs and monologues during a visit to the Day Club on the Market Square.

Above: Comedian Claude Dampier behind the bar of the Wheatsheaf at Daventry, a favourite hangout for servicemen stationed hereabouts, during at morale-boosting visit. Casting his professional eye on his technique is Alec McGill.

Left: While American servicemen at the Plough Hotel rest centre may not have understood Cyril Fletcher's Odd Odes, or his strangled catchphrase "Dreemin' of Thee".....

Above .... convalescing British troops, in their hospital blues, did and acquired his autograph on free theatre tickets, a gift from the Chronicle & Echo.

Right: Northampton's own stars, Bertha Wilmott and husband Reg, one time licensees of the Spinney Hill hotel, undertook many wartime tours with E.N.S.A.

Above: The Radio Gardener, Mr C.H. Middleton who lived at Lois Weedon, became a star in his own right in the wake of the Dig for Victory campaign. Here he meets a group of A.T.S. drivers.

Right: Women in a local munition factory crowd round to get the autograph of orchestra conductor Stanford Robinson after a Workers Playtime programme. The girl on the right has obviously got an American serviceman boyfriend! Several of the women are wearing their hair in the Victory Roll, a style designed to be achieved without the aid of hairpins.

Left: Vic Oliver, a concert pianist and violinist, hit the radio bigtime with Ben Lyon and Bebe Daniels in the wartime comedy show "Hi Gang! " He was Churchill's son-in-law, having married the Prime Ministers daughter. He met this group of office workers during a Workers Playtime visit to Daventry.

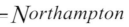

Left: The smash hit radio programme of the day was ITMA, "It's That Man Again", starring Tommy Handley. A long list of catchphrases from the show went into everyday usage, "Don't forget the diver!", "After you Claude. No, after you, Cecil!", "Giv'im d'woiks, Lefty!", Mrs Mopp's "Can I do yer now, sir?", the bibulous Colonel Chinstrap's "I don't mind if I do", and the sinister voice down the telephone, "Dis ees Funf speakink!" On one of his visits to the town Tommy Handley attended the childrens Saturday morning club at the Exchange Cinema where he led the audience in the Gaumont British Club song.

Below: The Home Guard, meanwhile, was going from strength to strength. Proper uniform, instead of khaki denims, proper weapons, and efficient training, had brought them out of the Dad's Army phase. A demonstration of stripping and reassembling a Sten Carbine light machine gun, at Abington Park, absorbs watchers. This simple gun, with only 59 components, was at first laughingly referred to as "the gas lighter", but soon gained the respect of the men.

The array of armaments paraded by the Home Guard at a drumhead service held at the County Ground in connection with a National Day of Prayer in September of 1943 is interesting. Lined up on the left are Northover projectors, christened "drainpipe artillery" by the Home Guard when they first arrived during Christmas 1941. In front of them are a row of spigot mortars. The wheeled devices being pulled by the men are Smith guns, a mobile mortar which could be thrown on its side so that one wheel formed the traverse and the other provided protection from falling shrapnel. It was capable of throwing a 10lb bomb over 1,000 yards.

Left: Every town and village in the county had its Home Guard unit. This is the Towcester division on parade.

Left Below: The crack dispatch riders of the 12th Battalion (Northampton) Home Guard ride past Col. P. Lester Reid at the County Ground. 20 riders with their own machines were selected to deliver signals from HQ. They were instructed, if captured, to either eat the message or drop it in the petrol tank, when the fuel would dissolve the ink! They usually finished their parade in a Victory-V formation.

Below: Lady Mountbatten (centre) visited the Northampton Voluntary Aid Detachment at the Town Hall where she watched nurses of the St. John Ambulance Brigade at work.

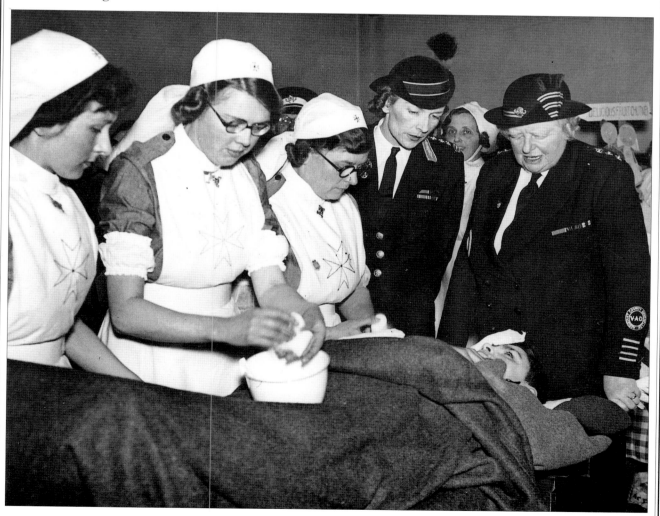

Left: Another royal visitor was Queen Geraldine of Albania who tried Northamptonshires traditional skittle game at a fete near Towcester.

Above: A famous film star put in an appearance for Wings for Victory Week in May 1943. It was the R.A.F. Wellington bomber "F for Freddie". With over 50 bombing raids to it's credit, it had featured in a popular film "Target for Tonight".

Right: Wings for Victory Week was followed almost immediately by Salute the Soldier Week, in June of 1943. It once more brought a display of tanks to the Market Square, and the inevitable horde of children.

Above: Men and women from the armed forces, as well as contingents from Civil Defence and all the auxiliary services gathered in the Market Square before parading through the town as part of the weeks events.

Left: Speaking at the opening of Salute the Soldier Week was Lt-General Sir Kenneth Anderson, by now Commander in Charge of Eastern Command, famous for his leadership of the British First Army in North Africa.

Right: In 1943 refugees were still arriving in England. A party of Polish and French Jews arrive at Northampton's Castle Station. Most went on to enlist in the Free French or Polish forces.

Are we downhearted? Certainly not! A party of Northampton A.T.S. girls at one of their regular get-togethers in a local school hall.

Left: Another happy band. Wives and sweethearts of local servicemen met each week at the Wedgewood tea-rooms in Abington Street to exchange news of their partners and to keep up morale.

Above: Similarly, wives and mothers of local men held as prisoners of war by the enemy, met to exchange news. Each table carried the name of a POW camp and relatives with men in those camps gathered there to swap snippets of information.

Above: In the latter part of 1943 a contingent of the Czechoslovak Armoured Brigade was stationed in the town. These tough troops had just returned from a three year stint in the Middle East. Here to meet them came the President of Czechoslovia Dr. Benes (centre).

Left: Among the Czechs was Corporal Emil Koroschenko, claimed to be the worlds strongest man. At a demonstration at the Roadmender Club six men bent a steel bar over the bridge of his nose! In this photograph he is bending an old penny in half in his teeth.

Right: The boys of the 41st Northampton Army Cadets stand to attention, even though their uniforms may be at ease! Lt-Gen. G St. G. Robinson inspects them at a camp at Overstone.

Above: A Northampton contingent of Sea Cadets meets with the approval of the Duchess of Gloucester during an inspection.

Right: Creches were set up to care for young children while their mothers were engaged in war work. First the washday chores for this group of little girls ....

Far Right: ....then the washing must be hung out to dry.

Left: Prayers before the lunchtime sandwiches.

Below: The boys preferred to get dirty in the sandpit!

Right: Lilford Hall, near Thrapston, was taken over as a convalescent home where servicemen recovered from stress or injury. Nurses wave off another party of recovered soldiers as they return to their units.

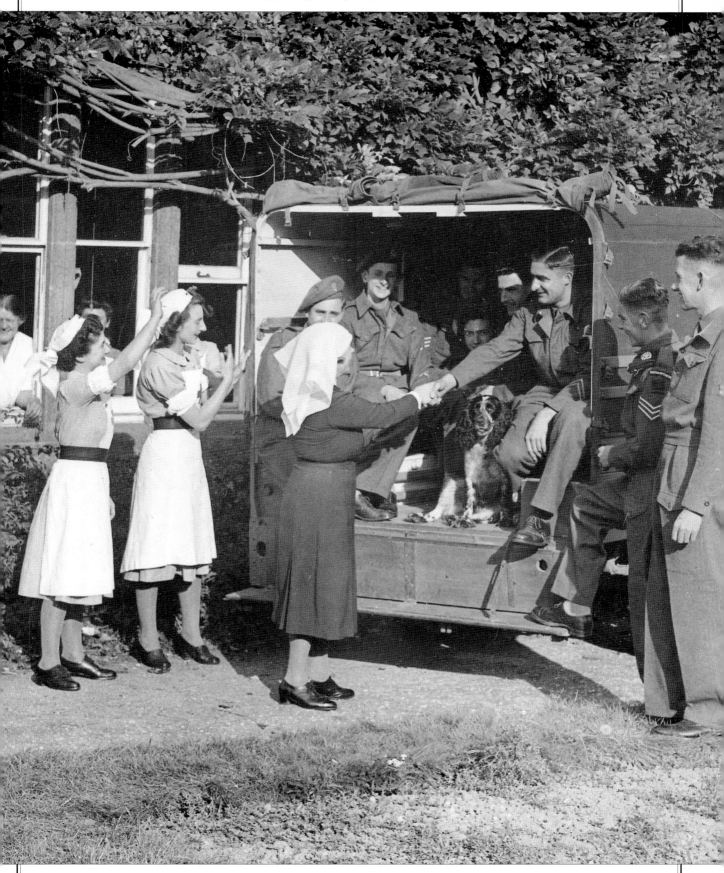

Left: Outings of various kinds were arranged for war-wounded soldiers, like this visit to the pipe chamber of the Savoy Cinema where the manager indicates some of the smallest pipes of the mighty Compton organ.

Below Left: Happy to be back in England, these convalescing soldiers have decorated their bus for a visit to Northampton.

Below: Lilford Hall was also home to recovering ex-prisoners of war repatriated by the Germans. A.T.S. girls from nearby camps visit the unit for a dance, part of the rehabilitation programme.

Left: Driver Joe Gordon was re-united with his wife, daughter Sheila aged seven and his son aged two, who he had never seen, after being repatriated from an Austrian POW camp.

Below: In service units, dotted throughout the local countryside, women did their bit helping to keep the vehicles running. Maintaining the British version of the U.S. Sherman Firefly tank was heavy work for women.

Above: The ubiquitous jeep was returned in large numbers to a Northampton M.T. unit from camps throughout the area for repair and maintenance.

Above: Close to Silverstone village was a large and active operational airfield. Sir Harry Brittain, on a visit, was shown the switchgear that controlled the landing lights. The distinctive pattern of runways and dispersal areas that later became the Silverstone motor racing circuit can be clearly seen.

Right: Many British, Allied, and German planes crashed in the Northampton area. This Flying Fortress narrowly avoided the village of Walgrave when it failed to make it back to base after limping home from a bomber raid.

Left: In March 1943 King George VI and Queen
Elizabeth visited Northampton and Kettering, arriving by
train.

Below Left: At a reception at Northampton Town Hall
they were left alone and unattended by the mayor and
corporation officials, much to their royal embarrassment,
as they waited to be invited to their seats. On the left is
Lord Trent with mayoress Mrs Lees.

Below: At Kettering the King and Queen met members of
the Auxiliary Fire Service.

"Is your journey really necessary?" asked the posters all over the place. In line with the drive to avoid unnecessary travel, a programme of Holidays at Home was planned. So starved of entertainment was everyone by high summer 1943 that age-old Punch and Judy attracted a huge crowd of adults as well as children on the Racecourse.

Right: A make shift tent kept this group of lads amused on the Racecourse in the summer of 1943.

Above: On June 6th, 1944, the allies launched D-Day and, in a final act of desperation, the Germans launched their first flying bombs against England. Just a month later, in July, one of the "doodlebugs" fell at Creaton, narrowly missing the village pub, the Bricklayers Arms. Landing in an orchard, it did only superficial damage.

Left: The summer of 1944 brought drought and severe restrictions on the use of water. Despite the National Fire Service pumping millions of gallons from the River Nene into reservoirs, housewives were forced to fill enamel baths and other receptacles during the brief time the mains were turned on. The needs of army camps and airfields, a population vastly increased by evacuees, and the need to maintain food production on the farms, added to the difficulties.

Below: If the summer was hot, the following winter made up for it. The River Nene at South Bridge was frozen over as girls of the Northampton Sea Rangers launched their new boat, the "Ajax", for it's first trial in January of 1945.

The Home Guard, which had done such a splendid job since the days of the L.D.V., was no longer felt to be necessary and December 3rd, 1944, was declared Stand Down day. A huge parade was held in London, to which Northamptonshire battalions sent representatives. In Northampton a parade was held on the Market Square before Col. P. Lester Reid. A sidelight of this event was when Mr. Thomas Walter of Albion Place was called forward for special commendation. Aged 88, he had knocked 20 years off his age when signing on to defeat the 65 year old barrier. He was the oldest active Home Guard in Britain.

Above: On May 7th 1945 Germany surrendered. The next day was designated VE-Day, Victory in Europe. Crowds of people on the Market Square look almost stunned by the happy news.

Left: The New Inn, on the Kettering Road, improvised makeshift floodlights and crowds gathered to dance and sing with the locals in the road.

Right: In St. Michaels Road the residents brought out all the old furniture that they could find and broke it up to improvise a bonfire in the middle of the road. The scars remained for many long years afterwards!

In Gladstone Terrace, a small community that never needed much excuse for a street party, celebrations began in earnest. A more sedate moment came when the street was visited by the mayor and mayoress, Ald. Sydney and Mrs. Strickland.

Left: Early morning revellers on the Market Square. A measure of wartime "make-do-and-mend" can be seen in the darned ladder in the girls stocking, whose knee appears from behind the centre bicycle rider.

Below Left: Crowds gathered, too, on the Market Square to await the arrival of the band of the Northamptonshire Regiment that had toured the town collecting a vast procession of celebrating followers.

Above: Blackout was abandoned and the window coverings that had been so essential were rapidly torn down. The thick black paint that had obscured the windows at Manfield Orthopaedic Hospital was hurriedly scraped off by a band of willing volunteers.

Northampton market took on a new look, even though there was still no let-up in strict rationing, as stallholders stayed open into the evening and lit their lamps again.

Below: It was decided that there was to be a general election on July 5th, 1945. Winston Churchill, who since May had headed a "caretaker" government replacing the wartime coalition, visited the area in a pre-election campaign on 25th June 1945. He addressed voters at Daventry from the seat of a Humber convertible car.

Right: It was noted that he looked worn from his wartime exertions.

Left: At Whittlebury this elderly gentleman declared his patriotism by riding to meet Churchill bearing the Union flag.

Right: The prospective Conservative candidate for Kettering was Lt-Col. John Profumo, seen here on a campaign visit to a local shoe factory and helping an army officer to select his demob shoes. Profumo later became infamous for his part in the Christine Keeler and Mandy Rice-Davies affair.

Below: Also visiting the locality was Clement Attlee, leader of the Labour party, with his wife.

Left: Police supervised the loading of ballot boxes on to Corporation buses for delivery to the centres where votes would be counted.

Below: It took three weeks to gather the votes and do the counting. On July 26th a late-night crowd gathered outside the Chronicle & Echo building on the Market Square as the results were posted in the windows. To the surprise of the world, in view of Churchill's wartime record, though perhaps not to observers in Britain, a Labour government was elected and Attlee became Prime Minister. Thus Churchill didn't see the end of the war and the victory for which he was so largely responsible as Prime Minister.

Above: In the early days of August two hydrogen bombs were dropped on Japan and, on the 14th of that month Japan surrendered. Next day was declared VJ Day and, as far as Northampton was concerned, was virtually a re-run of VE Day. In expectation of the event fireworks had once more gone into production and limited supplies were on sale. Rockets, flares and other fireworks were let off on the Market Square and from the top of the fountain.

Above: Soon war-weary servicemen started returning for demobilisation, arriving at the Castle Station en route for the Drill Hall or several more "demob centres" in the locality.

Left: Happy to see the back of army life, they were faced at the Castle Station with the welcome sign, "This way for Civvy street".

Right: A grinning soldier gets his demob kit at the Drill Hall, a civvy suit (single breasted with no turnups, sleeve buttons, or lapel button-holes, for they were still banned by clothing regulations). shoes, and a choice of hat, either cloth cap or trilby.

Left: At Gladstone Terrace Corporal A.R. Norman gets a warm welcome from friends and neighbours as he makes his way home to No. 16. He had spent a long period in a German POW camp.

Below: A hug from his wife and family, too as he is almost overwhelmed by neighbours.

*Above: The town's boot and shoe industry lost no time in resuming
normal production, displaying to the world the many types of
footwear designed and supplied to the armed forces during the
war. Lt-Gen. Sir John Brown (left) examines a special army boot
with the mayor Ald. Sydney Strickland at a display in the
Guildhall in August of 1945.*

Right: Once the war was over there was a great curiosity about the Northamptonshire service establishments that had been forbidden territory during the war. The airfield close by Silverstone village threw its gates open to the public on September 15th, 1945, with aircraft and services on display. Crowds came to get a close look at bombers like this Lancaster.

Above: A row of Spitfire fighters were also on show at Silverstone.

Below: Queues formed to go inside the Lancaster. At last families could see the cramped and uncomfortable conditions in which their sons had gone to war!

Above: Many families had nothing to celebrate, with loved ones killed or maimed. In October of 1945 a more sober week of thanksgiving was held. Once more an aircraft, a Spitfire, was assembled on the Market Square, but this time merely as a backdrop to the dais.

Right: The final preparations had to be squashed in between the market stalls.

*Thanksgiving Week was opened by the Marquess
of Exeter, backed by representatives of all the
services. Music for the service was provided by
the band of the Northamptonshire Regiment.*

Right: The mayor of Northampton, Ald. Sydney Strickland and Mr. H. Talbot-Butler (right) are shown the powerful engine of the Spitfire.

Below: Marquess of Exeter, Lord Lieutenant of Northamptonshire is greeted by the mayor Ald. S. Strickland.

Left: Factories were getting back to normal, even the small ones. In Flore a small unit run by Mrs Maxwell-Channell which, during the war, had produced high velocity incendiary bombs, turned to the production of electric kettles.

Right: Northamptonians just couldn't wait to get rid of one ugly reminder of the war, the street shelters. In January 1946 the "Basher", a huge iron weight which was swung into the brickwork by a crane, arrived in town to demolish them. It is seen here at work in Stanley Road, St. James's End.

Below: Unlike the shelters built in the early days of the war, these were robust and required a lot of effort to destroy them. Most, like this one in Greenwood Road, came apart in huge chunks.

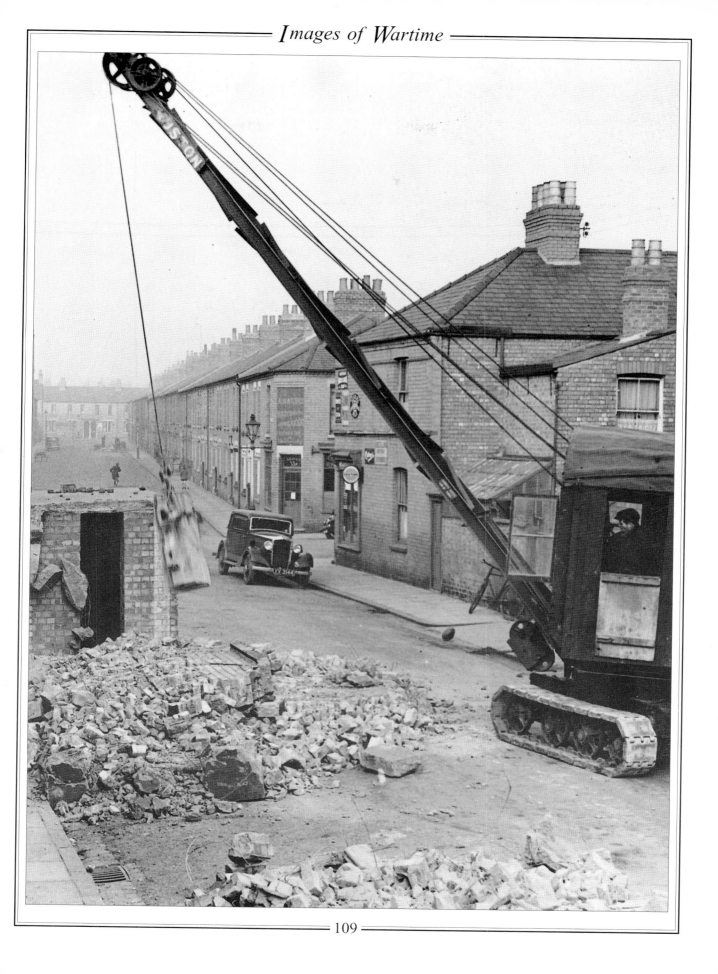

Left: Masses of war-surplus materials came on the market as government sales took place to clear the stock. Over 7,000 vehicles, tractors, cranes, earth-movers, bowsers, and airfield maintenance vehicles, came up for sale at Spanhoe 'drome, near Kettering.

Below: A special parade was held to mark the return home of contingents of the Northamptonshire Regiment from service in the Far East. At least in their home town they were not "the forgotten army". They paraded in their distinctive "bush hats" in front of the Town Hall.

Below Left: To honour the achievements of the Northamptonshire Regiment, the Freedom of the Borough was awarded to them on 8th June, 1946, giving them the right to march through the town with flags flying and bayonets fixed. The ceremony took place on the Market Square.

Left: The choir of All Saints church led the service before a dais bearing the battle honours of the regiment.

Below: The occasion was marked by a huge hoarding placed on the front of the Chronicle & Echo building and illuminated at night.